Meditations at Midnight

Poetry and Prose

gary jansen

LOYOLA PRESS.
Chicago

LOYOLAPRESS.
www.loyolapress.com

ISBN 978-0-8294-5888-6

Library of Congress Control Number: 2023944990

Printed in the United States of America.

23 24 25 26 27 28 29 30 31 32 Versa 10 9 8 7 6 5 4 3 2 1

for Grace, Eddie, and Charlie,
the moon and the stars:
a book in five parts.

VIA DOLOROSA

A SMALL THING

The coldest night of the year.
A transparent moon hangs in the sky.
Beneath it, a garden like the one where your
ancestors played.

You cry into your hands.
There are whispers in the dark
and the spirit of another watching over you.

You remember a young child,
walking in the cool breeze by the sea
with his mother and father.
There were twelve rocks in the boy's pocket,
small ordinary stones taken from the shore,
from the streets.

You remember the child crying when he lost one.
The twelfth is missing, the boy said.
Now there are only eleven.
His father beside him, touching his hair.
His mother holding him in her arms,
a prescient embrace.
Her neck like the smell of roses.

The deep air, a waking dream.
A cup before you.

Is this yours? a voice asks, trying to lift it.
So heavy for such a small thing.
Don't touch it. Put it down. You don't want this.
This is not how things were supposed to be.
There was a promise of something else.

Your stomach burns. A strange sweat on your lips.

Please, you say. *I cannot bear it.*

Then, a quiet voice.
The wind, the perfume of flowers, touches your hair.
You can. You must.

You see a stone moving, giving way to light.

Your will, you cry.

I will.

HELLO, OLD FRIEND

Moonlight pours through a web of olive trees.

Flares in the distance, torches
like stars in outstretched hands.

I have been wondering when you would arrive,
old friend—weak chin, sallow face, bony arms.
You look older than I remember.
At supper you were a boy with a secret,
silver-eyed and restless.
Now, you stare at me like a scarecrow after harvest.

Something has always trailed you.
I felt it again earlier tonight.
I feel it now.
Even as you move closer,
I feel its presence feather your heart.

You have always been a beam of splinters.
You have punctured the skin
of so many who drew near you.
I have known about this for some time.
And when there was talk of mercy,
I would watch your tiny looks,

almost imperceptible,
the subtle grimace,
a narrowing of the eyes,
a quiet laugh in the back of your throat.
You always kept your distance.

But, tonight,
you are the only brother
to touch me.
You are the last.
And with a kiss.
Dry.
Punctured.
The first nail.

They take me.

CROWS

Voices emerge out of darkness,
and the scent of wine and vinegar.
You stand before them.
They pant like hungry dogs.

No humor. No irony.
Circles of shadow frame disjointed faces,
a room of cracked mirrors,
fear reflected a thousand times.

Dark halos, lips twisted,
like those who speak
from both sides of their mouths.
They talk of revolution and peace.

They know nothing.

The same angel of the desert
who did this to Pharaoh
whispers in their ears tonight:
Harden your hearts.

There is nothing that can be said.
No truth. This is all just making motions.

A mock trial. A conspiracy of cowards.
They feud among themselves.

Their anger is so boring.

They tear down what God created.
You will rebuild.

OMEN

You loved him before you knew him.
He, fashioned for loyalty,
was always by your side.
It was hard to get rid of him.

Both of you would rise before the cock crowed,
and explore the hills before dawn,
watching the ascension of the sun
over this land of tombs.
Together, you would recall cloudless
evenings walking past the portico,
the overturned boats resting for the night.

Once, the flutter of noisy birds.

An omen, you said.

Of what? he asked.

In time.

The two of you talked for hours.
When you needed to be alone, he wouldn't leave.

You must go.

I won't leave you.

Now, black winds.
Night has fallen.
Your hands are cold.
Your heart is sleepless.
You wait, knowing he won't come.

In the distance, the crowing of early dawn.

WHAT IS TRUTH?

I thought he would be taller,
but he is just a man.

Let it be done.

NEIGHBORS

He stands before you,
a hollow man in hollow armor.
He is the same age.
You stare into his empty eyes.

You have no power except what has been given to you.

The sound of lashes on your back
like birds screaming.
Blood runs from the corners of your mouth.
His blows burn like a bush on fire.
He breaks your nose.

Hands raised, you look to the sky.
You close your eyes,
and try not to hear the thunder.

The crowning. The sovereignty of pain.

Blood from his dirty fingers mixes with yours.
You are now brethren as he lifts you to your feet
in a devil's embrace.

As boys, you didn't know each other,
but looked at the same stars
and, in the summertime, prayed for rain.

A GIRL

Bruised skin. Purple fingers. Dust coats your mouth.
Heavy air hangs on you like another layer of skin.
At noon, the sun barely casts a shadow.

This wood is so heavy.
How can wood be this heavy?

A voice. Not just one voice. Countless.

The unfaithful. The murderers.
The liars. The lukewarm.
The poor. The sick. The lonely.
They are all in your head, all on your back.

So many. How is this possible?

Your shoulders burn, and you remember a girl
walking in the cool breeze of a summer morning.
She vanished from sight,
leaving behind the smell of lavender.

She has returned. She knows where to take you.

Follow her.

THIRST

Dogs sniff the streets.
Blood.

You fall.
A soldier strikes your leg.
You cannot move, the weight is too much.

All this frightens the man with the boyish face,
who stares as if into the eyes of demons.
A soldier seizes him.

Carry this.

He picks up the heavy wood,
struggles, but bears the weight.

You look into his eyes. The color of desert sand.

You think of water but know you will not drink.

HARBINGERS

This crowded street.
You see them through matted hair.
They squawk like blackbirds,
thirteen of them,
weeping, anxious voices,
performing a dance
to ease you into the next life.

Don't cry for me, you say.
The world keeps God away.
Weep because of that.

THE PROMISE

As a boy you played in places like this,
cracked earth and arthritic-looking rocks.

An old man, a collector of bones, would pulverize
the dead, mixing the meal with oil and malachite
to paint astrological charts on the skins of lambs.

He told you that one day you would become a king.
It is written in the stars, he said.

You stood fixed, looking at his
cart of curiosities—balls of crystal, amulets like eyes,
butterflies pinned to bits of cypress.

Now you see traces of clouds.
A knife, a rope, nails, and a hammer.
You used these tools in your father's workshop
to join wood together.

Now, a crude carpenter joins you to a beam.
When the iron pierces your flesh,
you think of a dove descending from the sky,
whispering something in your ear.

The promise of honey, olives, milk.
The promise of love.

FATHER AND SON

You look into his eyes.
You never had a son, but you wish now
you could be a father to this man.
He was unexpected.
You thought you were journeying alone,
didn't expect this chosen one
to be your companion into the next life.

God of surprises. God of mercy.

My son, today we travel light.

REMEMBERING THEN AND NOW

You are a boy.

You remember the darkening room.
and the hissing,
like steam from a kettle.

You could not see it
    but you could feel it
        moving over the floor,
            inching ever closer.
You knew you were going to die.

But then an open door,
a bright light,
and she struck,
crushing the head of the asp with her foot.

The tail flashed.
Panting, your mother said, "The first of many."

You look upon her now,
years later,
Mother of your Heart,
Enemy of Serpents.

She holds her hands aloft.
She asks God to deliver you back into her arms.
Soon, she will hold you;
soon, you will feel her embrace.

But now, you bless her,
and give her to another.

She is no longer yours.
She belongs to everyone.

AND THE THUNDER SAYS

Ravens fly overhead, black feathers like smoke.
Like a ghost in a tree, something quiet is watching you.
The one from the desert
has his hands around your throat.
He squeezes.
You have the desert in your mouth.
You thirst.

You raise your head to the sky and see rivers of
suffering eyes,
a multiplication of sorrows.
In this savage stillness, you feel it all.
It burns like lightning.
From your parched heart you call out to your Father,
and the dark shadow disperses like fire thrown into
the sea.

Then the thunder says,
He who was living is now dead.
We who are living are now dying.

A BEGINNING

This desert sunset turns the sea to wine.
Your mother caresses you one more time,
then hands you over to the one
who would visit you in the dark,
ask questions, listen.
He carries your answers around with him,
in his heart that now beats,
in the shroud he holds,
in the cloth he wraps around you,
like the one from long ago
when angels heralded your arrival.

A slab of rock for a bed,
a stone for a pillow,
in this restless darkness you sleep.

But not for long.

VIA VITAE

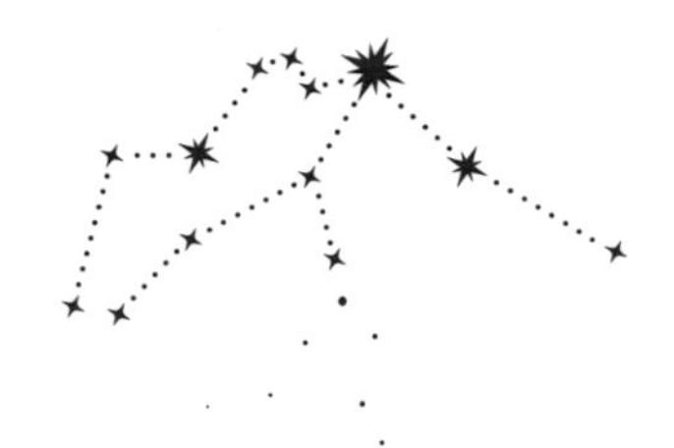

I

The old man and the boy were walking through a park.

"See those two trees over there?" said the old man.

"Yes," said the boy.

"See the distance between them? See how their branches almost touch each other? *Almost,* but never do?"

"Yes."

"The tree on the lcft *adores* the tree on the right. And I'm pretty sure the tree on the right feels the same way about the tree on the left. They can't stop looking at each other. Did you hear what I said?"

The boy, startled, answered, "Yes."

The old man sighed.

"No matter how much they yearn to be closer to each other they can never touch. They can never touch each other's happiness. They never can touch each other's suffering. If one gets sick, the other one can only watch, can't help. They are locked apart from each other forever."

"Unless lightning knocks one of them over onto the other," said the boy.

"Yes, you're right," said the old man.

They stood together silently for a while, the wind blowing the branches of the trees. The old man smiled.

The boy looked up. "This makes me sad and angry," he said. "What are you smiling about?"

"Don't be sad," said the old man. "Yes, the branches of the trees can never touch. They can never hug. But if you go below the surface, the roots of these two separate trees are entwined and entangled. What they yearn for above, they experience deep below. We can't see it, but they share one life. What happens to one, happens to the other."

The boy thought for a moment, nodded, and said, "I'm hungry."

"Me too. Let's go."

II

The old man spoke:

"You are like a person who has waited his entire life to see a painting in a museum. You finally get your chance to travel, to go to this place you have been dreaming about. You enter, you find where the painting is, and you walk to the room. Before you enter, you take a deep breath. You cross the threshold. The painting is to your right, and you automatically move as close to it as you possibly can without touching it. Certainly, if the curator and not the security guard was in the room, you would be told to step away. But you are here. You are looking at the painting you've waited your whole life to see.

"Something catches your eye, though, and you turn around and see another man, a distinguished and gentle man standing in the middle of the room observing the same painting as you are, but from a distance. He must be viewing you too because you're so close to it, you've become a part of the painting yourself. You are intrigued and you want to see what he sees, so you move closer to him. Standing shoulder to shoulder (you're a bit shorter than he is), you look around and you see the painting you've always wanted to see, but from a different perspective. It is beautiful, but so are all these other paintings in the room—the paintings you missed."

III

An old man stood outside a church in the middle of a busy city and watched as passersby went about their daily business. Many were shuffling off to work, others were walking around in shorts carrying newspapers and brown paper bags, and still others seemed lost and in need of directions. Around noon, the old man looked up at the tall steeple and fixed his gaze upon the thin iron cross that sat on the top. Every once in a while, a man on his way to lunch or a woman on her way to the drugstore for cotton balls would pause and look up too. If the person lingered for a moment, the old man would ask, "What is the Holy Spirit?" Many people said nothing and took his words as their cue to move on. Some said, "I don't know." Others said words like *God, Jesus, grass, smoke, fire, energy, a new line of sports shoes.* This went on for hours.

As the sun began to set, casting the street in the colors of Sri Lankan silk, and after hours of staring upward, his neck feeling stiff and pinched, the old man turned his gaze to the street. Walking toward him was a beautiful woman in a sundress. With the sun shining on her she looked as if she radiated phosphorus.

“What is Truth?” the old man asked.

Looking like an angel of God the woman smiled, raised her hand, her fingernails painted in Technicolor, and slapped his face with the strength of a small army.

“That’s the Truth,” she said, and walked away.

The old man, his cheek burning with the fire of angels, knew exactly what she meant.

IV

The old man posed a question to the group: if God were a tree, what kind of tree would he be?

Those in attendance thought about this, and after a few minutes of reflection, some of them began to speak:

"God is a huge oak tree because God is strong, and his roots are deep."

"God is a sycamore because I used to pray under one of those trees when I was a child."

"God is an elm tree because he gives me shade and because, well, I like elm trees."

"God is a banyan tree because it is the most magnificent tree I've ever seen. There is one by a monastery near my home. On weekends in autumn, in the moments between night and dawn, I will walk to that field and enter under its canopy. I sit there on one of the long arms close to the ground and listen to the geese fly overhead."

"I'm from Arizona and there aren't many trees where I live. God is a cactus."

"I don't really like trees—all the leaves you have to clean up in the fall. God's not a tree to me."

"I know someone said that the banyan tree is the most magnificent tree in the world, but I'm assuming that's only because he's never seen a redwood. I was in that forest some years back, and you'd be amazed at the size of these things. I mean, their trunks are as big as this room and some have been around for thousands of years. They stretch so high into the sky that you can't see where they end. That is God to me."

Jesus was sitting in the room at the time, though no one recognized him. When it was his turn to speak, he said, "God for me is like the Charlie Brown Christmas tree."

"You mean that skinny little thing in the cartoon?" asked someone.

"Yes. For me, God is fragile and naked, and most people pass him by without giving him much thought. The only people who know the beauty that lies within are children who don't know any better."

Someone eating grapes moaned, "Good grief."

VIA CORDIS

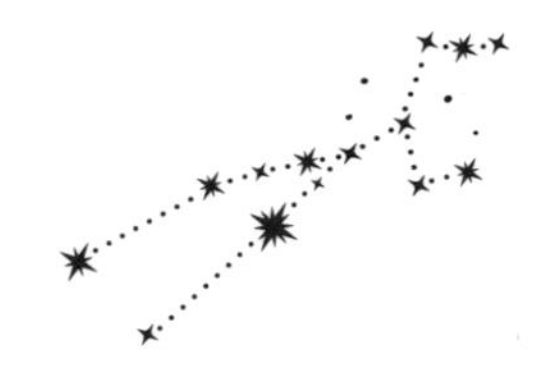

THE BEAUTIFUL EAR

It's true.
Her ear winked at me.
I know it sounds impossible.
I can't explain how it happened,
but I can tell you when it did.

I was sitting in a room full of strangers
I had known for almost a year,
everyone looking bored, or confused,
like cadavers, or the indignant images
on canceled postage stamps.

To my left, I heard a smile break
like a wave,
and I turned to see you
burst into the room
like St. Elmo's Fire,
burning green and orange, yellow and blue.

You started talking to a man
who looked like an unanchored buoy,
and then you tucked your hair,
brown and beautiful, behind your ear.

Someone opened a can of something or other.
Someone dropped a set of keys.
Someone else sneezed.
And that's when it happened,
that's when it happened!

O, winking ear, O, fleshy seashell,
How I want to press you against
my mouth and listen to your sea.

ART FOR ART'S SAKE

We gather on Wednesdays at a local coffee shop,
Harry, Peter, Sarah, myself—Claude's there too—
a group of writers who never write,
separate from the painters and sculptors at the next table
who haven't touched watercolors or clay in years.

We talk about past accomplishments:
trips to Europe; an article here and there;
a newsletter created, aborted, brought back to life,
then murdered by a computer virus.

In another booth, I watch a woman, maybe twenty-one,
whose hair, like an old high school sweetheart's,
is a mess of knots and frosted highlights,
rest her head against the coffee-stained walls.

And I sit listening to my friends,
who already have begun to fade from my memory,
as my hair thins, my belly grows soft, and I feel
the incarnation of a toothache
that pinches the back of my jaw.

INSOMNIA: A BLESSING

I admit it,
I drank the holy water,
but only because I was thirsty for you.

Moonlight penetrates your window,
and covers your face in nightlace.
Beautiful after-midnight webveil.

LEAVING TOMORROW

Twenty-three stories above the city,
the November sun sets beyond skyscrapers.

Time hangs still
in pink sunlight.

Delicate rays
streak your face and hair.

I watch you and the sun entwine,
giving life to twilight.

TUESDAY AT THE A&P

Hunched over from osteoporosis,
her smile has the same look as a jack o'lantern
in late November, one weak tooth decaying
in the middle of her mouth,
her cheeks soft and gaunt,
brown spots at the corners of her lips
from too much time in the sun.

I watch her tonight shopping for cat food,
and try to see her as she once was—
I erase those lines that cross her forehead like ivy,
gently scrape away and sand rough patches
below her eyes and around her nose,
and give her face a fresh coat of colonial
beige from Ace Hardware.
Then I fill out her hair
with a special horsehair paintbrush
I carry for just such an occasion and, finally,
reinforce the foundation,
replacing her spine with tempered steel—
it adds nearly four inches from floor-to-ceiling.

But when she sneezes and pulls a tissue
from inside her sleeve, my newly renovated house
of dreams reverts back to a pumpkin,
and I watch as she bends over, blows her nose,
and reaches for the fish-flavored, store-brand
can of cat food that gives Fluffy and Kitten diarrhea.

It is then that I see my grandfather,
dead these past six years,
standing behind her,
supporting her back,
applying just the right pressure to
keep her steady, and
whispering in her ear
some long ago story
about a kiss at Coney Island.

SIMIC COUNTRY

Coming in out of the rain last night,
I drank ten-year-old Black Label
with Pythagoras
while he explained on an abacus
all I ever wanted to
know about the transmigration of souls.

Archimedes and Galileo in tank tops and jeans
sat at the end of the bar,
discussing displacement and buoyancy
over shots of Jägermeister,
while one of Bach's sons,
the one with nine fingers,
played "Alexander's Ragtime Band"
badly on a Yamaha upright.

It was then I saw you standing,
half-hidden in lager light,
playing darts with a skeleton
with eyes of mother of coal,
and all I wanted to do was wrap you
and me in a cocoon of Syrian silk
and play strip poker until
we grew one set of wings.

BROOKLYN-BOUND R, 1998

They have said nothing to each other,
not since Union Square, when the accordionist
playing “Lady of Spain” moved between cars
in search of his father’s shadow.

That was when she turned away and expelled
all the air in her lungs upward, like a novice snorkeler.
He slouched in the orange side seat
like a weary foot soldier, some skin-pierced,
tattooed mercenary from the highlands of the Bronx.

You fold your *Times* in half like a paper flag—
Serbs continue killing women and children;
NATO prepares airstrikes to stop the Kosovo massacres.

He has attempted a verbal treaty.
She stares at the overhead advertisement
for birth control in Spanish,
deaf to his attempts at a peaceful accord.

When the doors open at Whitehall Street South Ferry,
she seems prepared to walk out of negotiations.

You see she is crying,
and you quickly return to Yugoslavia,
where snow has begun falling in the mountains.

A paragraph later you lower your paper like a drawbridge,
and watch the doors close behind them.
Through the unusually clear subway window
you watch as she throws
her arms around
her enemy,
closes her eyes,
and mouths to herself,

I am so in love, I am so in love.

ELEGY

As soon as you were born, he loved you
like an unsolvable equation or the remembered taste
of sausage and cashews during a famine.

Your early arrival forced a sudden exile,
like an unseen swell capsizes a lifeboat in calm seas.
And yet, in your restlessness,
his pilgrim heart found rest.

So strange to think he shares the earth with so many,
this solitary figure who loved only one woman,
a master-of-all trades, jack of none,
who still locates missing keys in your dreams.

His crossing must have been disorienting,
a refugee wandering
through a field of blackbirds,
or a clown with hair on fire,
parachuting into a desert,
coasting through the sky,
a lost star.

Peering through your window that morning,
you watched him smoke Parliaments

as he surveyed your home,
making notes in the margins of his memory,
contemplating an eternity of projects left undone.

That last cigarette was the best he ever had.

And as you watched him drive away,
his final smoke ring drifted high toward a tree,
grew small,
and came to rest
around the head of a caterpillar
with the sleepy morning eyes
of a risen Christ.

VIA MEMORIA

FOLLOW THE THREAD

Late one night in the fall of 1996, I was walking through the narrow, fog-covered, cobblestone streets of Prague in the Czech Republic. I was a homeless traveler at the time, having recently been evicted from a friend's apartment after a silly comment I made escalated into a full-blown argument and a case of hard feelings. Trying to save as much money as possible before I hopped a train the next day to Krakow, Poland, I had opted not to spend the night in one of the city's many run-down hostels, where the walls were thin, the clientele high and obnoxious, and where you could catch gonorrhea just by looking at a doorknob. Instead, I chose a more hygienic alternative. I decided to walk the bridges and avenues of the city at night, and if I needed to nap, I would do so in a doorway or on the steps of a church or in the waiting room of the train station.

Though Prague was not as manic as New York City, people were out in the streets at all hours of the night, drinking and partying. Old Town, for me the most beautiful part of the city, with its mixture of medieval, gothic, and baroque architecture, was bubbling with musicians, artists, and lost souls in search of someone to talk to. I could have used someone to talk to as well, but unfortunately, I didn't speak Czech. I was just another linguistically challenged American stray dog rambling through a former Communist country with an oversized backpack and a Eurail pass (worthless in any former Eastern Bloc countries at the time). Yet as I walked through the city, feeling a bit like a character in an Albert Camus novel, I was surprised to meet a few wanderers who spoke decent English. I listened to their stories of haunted saints and lost lovers with wooden teeth, and their dreams of visiting America or moving to Japan to open an import-goods shop.

One man, who smelled of wine and tobacco, pulled me aside, pointed to the sky, and told me that the atmosphere in Prague was different than in any other place in the world—that if the clouds are exactly right, the color red turns black in the moonlight. He held up a red silk glove before me and told me to look carefully. I didn't have the heart to tell him it still looked red to me and that maybe, just maybe, he was color-blind. Instead, I told my newfound friend of my self-imposed exile, of my pursuit of God, that I had been stalking the Old Man for years and had tracked him down to this very place. "He is evasive," I told him with a bit of madness in my speech. "Keep your eyes open; he could be anywhere." He just smiled and laughed. "You won't find God here."

I walked for most of the night between Old Town and New Town. Sometimes I would sit on the cobblestones of the Charles Bridge and stare at the statues of saints that lined the walls and wish they could talk and tell me what they had seen over the centuries—blue-jeaned lovers strolling beneath the stars, Nazis crossing the bridge in tanks, Russians with their rifles and cigarettes, telling dirty jokes and spitting into the river. My feet hurt. I was tired and wild-eyed, and a little bit dehydrated from drinking Pilsner Urquell for the last twenty-four hours (which was cheaper to buy than bottled water and it alleviated hunger), but, eventually, the morning arrived without incident, and I watched the sun rise over the city, turning the streets from dark blue to miasma gray.

I had a few more hours to kill before leaving for Poland, so I bought a pastry and coffee somewhere. Afterward, as I was crossing the street near Wenceslas Square, someone hobbled and brushed past me, turned the corner, and disappeared before I could get a closer look.

Prague was filled with pickpockets, and instinctively I touched the butt of my pants before remembering my wallet was in my backpack. At the time, I had always prided myself on being aware of my surroundings, but I hadn't heard him approach at all. It was like he manifested out of nowhere. I was startled, and my heart was racing. I felt hot and flushed, and the ground beneath my feet felt spongy, as if I were standing in mud. The street was quiet, like the waking moments after your name is called in a nightmare, and I felt an intense desire to track whatever had startled me and see where he was going. When I had arrived in this land of cheap beer, beautiful women, schizophrenic architecture, dark fairy tales, and eerie-looking marionettes, I had been told, strangely enough, by a group of travelers from Australia, to "follow the thread," that the world is a dark labyrinth, and to find your way in life, you have to follow the thread.

Standing there in the street, I felt the windows of the buildings staring at me with suspicious eyes, and I became fully aware of how lonely and hungry I was. All I wanted to do was go home—my real home in New York—but that wasn't happening any time soon. My plane ticket back to the States was nonrefundable, and I couldn't make any changes; plus, I was supposed to meet a friend in Paris in two weeks, and I couldn't just leave her high and dry. Since my train to Poland didn't leave until around noon and with nothing else to do that morning, I decided to follow whatever it was that had incarnated itself in front of me. "Follow the thread," I said to myself and turned the corner.

I soon saw a man in what looked like a ragged, headless bear suit, just some inebriated, limping circus performer who I was sure was on his way home to an angry, tired wife with a pair of sharp garden shears in her hands. I followed him for a few blocks until he unexpectedly turned into a church, its façade blackened by years of Communism, soot, and dirty rain.

"What are you doing? You must be really bored to be following some old drunk," I said to myself, and began to walk away when that still small voice in my head—which had gotten me into considerable trouble over the years—said I should go inside.

What the hell? I thought. So, I did.

Ascending the stone steps, I opened the thick wooden door, entered, and stood in the nave. The church was quiet and dark, and a strong smell of burnt cabbage soup hung in the air. I heard faint tapping noises, the sound of heating pipes waking from hibernation. The man was nowhere to be seen. I was alone, and since I'm a sucker for old churches, I walked up the central aisle toward the altar, staring at the dark statues, gold-colored buttresses, and stained glass. I listened to the sound of my footsteps echoing off the plastered walls and wooden pews, and when I was just about underneath the hanging crucifix, I felt something touch my back.

I turned around expecting to see the man I followed into the church. But no one was there, and I felt a strange heat break over me. I was all pins and needles, and I looked down, thinking I had stepped on an exposed extension cord, but there was nothing beneath my feet except cold marble. Every nerve of my body was on high alert, and my skin exploded into gooseflesh.

"Je-sus Chriiiiist," I said out loud, "what is that?"

And just like that, the feeling disappeared.

I did an about-face and peered up at the ceiling and colored windows. I saw a statue of Saint Michael looking ready to kick some ass, wings unfurled, sword drawn, crushing the body of a demon. I looked at the giant crucifix above the altar. I stared into the eyes of the suffering wooden Christ and whispered, "Are you there, God? It's me, Margaret."

No answer. Then, to the right of the sacristy, something fell. The crash scared the bejesus out of me. I turned, ran down the aisle, out the door, and into the bright sunlight of morning.

Outside, I looked all around me and saw no one. The street was empty. I felt embarrassed and stupid. I also felt spooked but didn't know why. "Follow the thread, my ass," I said. I quickly walked away from the old church, adjusting my backpack, and looked at my watch. *Maybe I can get an earlier train,* I thought, and, tossing the damn thread to the street, I made my way across the city toward the train station.

MONSTERS AND GHOSTS

I was sixteen years old when the death rattle sounded in my parents' marriage. It would be another seven years before my mom and dad divorced, but, in the summer of 1986, something snapped like a marrowless bone, and the blue colonial house we lived in on the corner of Grand and Clinton was broken in two.

I spent a lot of time away from home that summer. When I wasn't at my job pumping gas at Tony and Vinnie's Automotive Shop on the south side of town, I was at the library reading books on vampires, monsters, and werewolves. There was something about fictional horror that made the real-life *Twilight Zone* of my family falling apart easier to accept. At night I read Stephen King's *Skeleton Crew.* This collection of short stories featured the novella *The Mist,* which is about a supernatural fog that envelops a small town, bringing out the worst in a group of people trapped in a supermarket. Although the story takes place in Maine, I couldn't help but imagine that a similar thick cloud of disaster and dread had somehow blanketed my hometown and, in particular, my home.

I devoured the stories in *Skeleton Crew* like they were potato chips. I moved on to King's novels: *Carrie, Salem's Lot, The Shining,* and *Cujo.* These books spoke to me in altogether new ways. Chief among them was my identification with the doomed protagonists, most of whom were outsiders and misfits. King's main characters were almost always screwed from the get-go. For whatever reason, Fate had decided to be cruel to these people, and that was that. Sometimes the good guys won, sometimes not. But in the end, Fate is powerful and, more often than not, the son-of-a-bitch came out on top.

As that summer drew to a close and the arguing at home increased, I noticed a newspaper article announcing the release of a new King novel, one that incorporated all the monsters from our nightmares. The novel was titled *It*—"It" being the evil under the bed, the ghost in the basement, the distorted face staring at you from your closet in the middle of the night, or the thing scratching at your window during a thunderstorm. "It" could also be that horrid clown at the old TSS department store in Oceanside that had scared the crap out of six-year-old me (he tried to give me a piece of gum—I screamed and ran for my life). Although I didn't realize it at the time,

"It" was also the monsters that manifested in my parents' disappointment, sadness, and anger.

Big, ugly monsters lurking in the attic are one thing. Little memory monsters perched on my parents' shoulders and whispering vitriol in their ears as we sat around the dinner table are another.

I preordered the book at a local B. Dalton's in East Meadow on Long Island. (This was in the days before Amazon.com, when you had to call a store or stop in and talk to a real person, usually exchanging words of excitement about an upcoming new novel from a favorite author. How quaint.) I spent the remainder of the summer and my first days back at high school fantasizing about King's new book, wondering how he was going to scare the hell out of me this time.

In the middle of September, I got a call that the new King book had arrived. I begged my mom to take me to the store so I could dig right in. She agreed, and we hopped into her car and drove for half an hour along traffic light-riddled Hempstead Turnpike. I don't remember exactly what the weather was that evening, but in the fiction of my memory, the drive looked something like a

Ray Bradbury dusk: sky the color of bruised pumpkins, crepuscular shadows that made the people on the streets look like phantoms, and, in the distance, what may have been a dark mist rolling in from the south.

I was in and out of the store in fewer than five minutes. In my hands I held a whopping doorstop of a book. The cover depicted a dark street. Emanating from the shadows was a paper boat, and green, reptilian fingers were reaching out of a sewer grate. King's name, printed in blood-red letters, dominated the jacket, hanging like a specter over the title. The book, which was more than a thousand pages, would turn out to be the longest I had ever read.

"That's a big book," my mom observed. I glanced over at her. She looked tired. Hollow. At 5'6", I was still just a bit shorter than she was. Even so, I found myself imagining that if I was really, really tall, looking down onto the top of her head, I would see that she had been cored like an apple.

"What's the first line?" she asked.

I remember sniffing the top of the book, something I always did in those days. I opened it and heard a little pop as the tight binding acknowledged my presence.

I read aloud.

"'The terror, which would not end for another twenty-eight years—if it ever did end—began, so far as I know or can tell, with a boat made of a sheet of newspaper floating down a gutter swollen with rain.'"

To this day I don't know what exactly it was about those opening lines, but something about them made me want to become a writer.

Somehow, my mom, whom I always suspected of being able to read minds, said, "You're going to be a famous writer one day." I closed the book. Her words lingered like cigarette smoke in the air. We were silent.

Her few choice words shifted something inside me. Twenty-odd years later, Penguin would publish my book *Holy Ghosts,* a memoir about growing up in a haunted house. And though I'm far from famous, I did become a writer, just as my mom predicted. In fact, I may have started writing in my head on the way home that evening. It was a story about a moment in time; there were no ghosts, no monsters, no sinister mists, and nothing to fear, just a mother and her son driving together down a suburban turnpike at twilight.

THE RE-BRAINER

Some years back, I was walking on a narrow cobblestone street off the Saint-Germain in Paris when I noticed a scruffy-looking individual kneeling in front of a café praying, or begging, inventively. He appeared to be in his forties and was dressed in black pants and a white shirt. His beard was unkempt, but his hair, which was thinning on top, was handsomely combed. His eyes were closed tight. He rocked gently back and forth, hands clasped in front of his heart.

I remember that it was late in the afternoon, and the city streets and cafés were beginning to fill with tourists. No one was paying this man any attention, and I certainly didn't intend to. But all my life I have been a magnet for misfits, madmen, and mendicants, and just as I was about to turn away, he opened his eyes, stared right at me, winked, and gave me an I'm-going-to-ask-you-for-money smile. He jumped to his feet with the athleticism of a young man, said something to me in French, and genuflected.

"I'm sorry, I don't speak French," I said.

"Ah, Americaaan." He stood up quickly and put out his hand. I shook it. Calloused and strong.

"Yes," I said.

"Me!" Slapping his chest, he said, "I lived in Brooklyn for seven years with my brother until he died."

When he said the word *died,* he clasped his hands, raised them to heaven, and said something again in French.

"I'm sorry," I said.

"What is your name?" he asked. His accent was French, and his English was perfect. I told him.

"Allow me to introduce myself. I am the Re-Brainer." He bowed again to expose the large bald spot on the crown of his head. There was a scab in the center.

"Re-Brainer?"

"Yes, I am the Re-Brainer because I am rethinking the world into a new existence. With my brain!"

"Is that how you hurt yourself?" I pointed to the drying wound.

"Ah," he said, stroking his chin. "Sometimes the spirit is so powerful I fall down!"

"What spirit are you talking about?"

He stuck out his chest, placed one hand on his heart, and raised his other high, pointing to the darkening sky. "I have not had a drink since my brother died seven years ago! I am talking about the Holy Spirit! The Holy Spirit! The Spirit that flows through you and me!"

I excused myself and began walking away from him.

"Do you pray?" he asked. I stopped.

"I do," I replied.

"I pray all the time! When I am walking, when I am thinking, when I am eating, when I am sleeping, when I am falling." He took a step closer to me and whispered in my face, "I am praying right now."

He may not have been drunk, but he smelled like cigarettes and needed a bath.

"Re-Brainer," I said, gently slapping him on the chest, "I rename you Brother Lawrence!"

"Brother Lawrence?"

"Yes, he was a monk who turned his life into a perpetual prayer. Everything he did he believed was a prayer. If he washed a dish, he offered that moment up to God."

He raised both arms in the air, and his smile nearly eclipsed his face. He was missing two teeth. "I am Brother Lawrence, the Re-Brainer! I am rethinking the world into existence! With my brain!"

I had not wanted to talk to the man when he first locked onto me, but I had to admit that now I was intrigued. Nonetheless, I checked to be sure my wallet was in my pocket, then asked, "How are you going to do that, Brother Lawrence, the Re-Brainer?"

"By praying!" He jumped up and down and started to dance in place.

"And your prayers are going to change the world?"

"They already have."

We talked for a few more minutes. About Brooklyn and Coney Island, about his brother, a janitor who died from cancer. About love, booze, cigarettes, and God.

I had quickly grown fond of the man, but it was getting late.

"Can I have your cigarettes?" he asked.

"Sure." I gave him the pack I was holding in my hand. Brown-papered Nat Shermans from the old store on Forty-Second Street in New York City. (I don't smoke anymore.)

"I have something for you," he said.

"What is it, Brother Lawrence, the Re-Brainer?"

"It is this." He pulled an artist's paintbrush from his back pocket. He put it in my hand. His eyes narrowed, and while I don't remember his exact words, he told me a story in hushed tones that went something like this. . . .

"This looks like an ordinary paintbrush anyone could buy, but this particular brush has a long and colorful history, of which you are now a part. Originally bought in Cleveland, Ohio, by a mother for her twenty-two-year-old son with dreams of being a world-renowned artist, the brush traveled in the young man's valise, first on a Greyhound bus from Lake Erie Downtown Station to

New York City. From there, Henri (for this was the young man's name) departed for Paris, flying nonstop from JFK to Charles de Gaulle airport. It was while studying under the auspices of the International Council for the Preservation of the Humanities that the young man met Antoine, a young vine grower from the Loire Valley with the uncanny ability of changing wine into water.

"Miracle? You may think so. 'A curse,' he called it. They became friends and drank Evian out of burgundy bottles on the banks of the Seine while pontificating on the role of the artist in society (or the lack of a role for an artist in present-day society). It was during a night of drunken tomfoolery that the young man's favorite paintbrush, which he always carried with him in the breast pocket of an old coat his father used to wear, was lost in a scuffle with some local boys from the Nord.

"Lying in the street for days, the brush was picked up by a vagrant street magician known in the cafés along the Saint-Germaine as Revoltaire. He used the brush as a disappointing substitute for the Magic Wand of Havana, a gift from his illusionist stepbrother in Cuba, to perform bits of sleight of hand and chicanery. While trying unsuccessfully to turn a belt into a spotted snake for a group of college students from Australia, this 'Street Christ' (as he was called by his one friend, Father Marcel of Notre Dame de Déception) lost his patience and threw the brush back into the street, where it was picked up eventually by a monkey named Pascal.

"Pascal's master, a one-handed accordionist and displaced Irishman named McGreevy, used the paintbrush on occasion as a conductor's baton when he whistled the melody of Edith Piaf's *'Effet que tu me fais'* (the only Piaf song he knew by heart) while Pascal danced his primitive ballet in the streets of the Latin Quarter for loose francs (this was before the currency switched to Euros). One night, as McGreevy and Pascal were walking home (home was a small studio above a chicken house in Montmartre), the brush fell out of a plastic bag and rolled down the long, steep steps photographed by countless romantics and known as the Stairway of Lovers, near Sacré-Coeur. Having traveled nearly one hundred and fifty steps, the brush at full velocity hit a high bump in a cobblestone street, and landed in a crate of blank videotapes that were being loaded onto a truck heading to the south of France for the Cannes Film Festival.

"Once the brush made it to the Riviera, it traveled through parts of Switzerland and Italy, carried for a time by the Seven Wandering Jews of Bratislava who had made a wrong turn in Slovakia. Then it changed hands from a pastry chef to a beautiful schoolteacher named Maman, to a young, crippled violinist named Sophie, to an old olive farmer in Sicily named Leo. From there it passed through several more hands—many with arthritis, moles, dry skin, broken fingernails, and gaudy gold rings—and landed in North Africa, where it fell into the possession of a group of Bedouins who mixed cactus wine with the dust of ancient pulverized stars, and used the brush to paint astrological charts on the skins of dead camels.

"Unfortunately—for these creations were reported to be the work of the great, great, great, great, great, great, great, great, great, great, great-grandson of one of the Magi who visited Christ at his birth—the brush was stolen by a Gypsy bandit as the Bedouins were trading their desert finds at an oasis for cans of sardines and chickpeas. It did, however, soon find its way to me. What transpired between myself and the Gypsy bandit, I cannot tell you, but you see now that we are all connected, by life, by death, by this brush. I am giving it to you. It is yours and it beckons you to paint!"

I stood with my mouth open. If it had been a hot midsummer night, not a cool April evening, I'm sure a fly would have flown down my throat. "I'm speechless. I don't know what to say."

"Say nothing," he said. "Paint!"

"I can't paint. I'm a writer."

"You will paint my story with words then."

"No one would believe it."

"Then paint words about prayer," he said.

I looked at the brush and at the eyes of this enflamed soul.

"I promise," I said.

"I am Brother Lawrence," he said, dancing. "The Re-Brainer. I am rethinking the world into existence. With my brain!"

I shook his hand, and he—a strange-smelling bear—hugged me. I said good-bye and walked off into the night.

A few blocks away I could have sworn I heard him call out: "Remember! Prayer!" But I couldn't be sure. I like to think he did.

I passed a couple sitting on the steps of a church kissing in the blue light of a spring night in Paris. I laid the brush at their feet, took out a pen, and wrote—or should I say, painted—in the small notebook I always carried with me two words: *Pray always.*

Brother Lawrence, the Re-Brainer, I have painted this story for you.

May God keep you safe.

ST. CECILIA AND THE BALLAD OF THE LONESOME TRAVELER

It is 2014, and I am in Rome on business. I sit alone beneath a white canopy at an outside table at the *Ristorante Sette Oche* in *Altalena* in Trastevere, eating my dinner. The people at the table next to me—a middle-aged couple in T-shirts—are talking about as much as I am. When they do speak, it's in German. I can't understand what they are saying, but there is no laughter and not a single smile. Still, I love them. I am in love with so much tonight—with my family back home, these strangers, the streets of brick and cobblestone, the façades of buildings with their chiseled angels and saints and gargoyles looking down upon me. A breeze blowing from the alleyway touches all of us in unison, weaving us together for a once-in-lifetime event now. I will never see these people again. Most will not know the sound of my voice, and I will not know their pain or lost desires, but I will carry something—like the memory of the small bump on the cheek of an old woman eating pineapple and drinking coffee a few tables away—of them wherever I go.

I have ordered chicken and prosciutto mixed with penne and Gorgonzola. When it arrives, the meal looks dry.

The salad is dry, too—a few lettuce leaves, a hiccup of radicchio, nothing else. None of it looks appetizing. Yet after the first bite, I realized, like so many other times in my life, looks can be deceiving. The food is delicious, and my mouth blooms with a perfect combination of meat, pasta, salt, pepper, olive oil, and cheese. Near perfection can be found in simple things like this and in how a man across from me pinches the bridge of his nose when he laughs, seated with his teenage son and drinking beer as the bare-shouldered girl beside them moves her pizza around her plate. The son checks his phone. His father sneezes. Gray hair curls at the base of the older man's neck. He laughs again. He pinches his nose. His son smiles and rechecks his phone. No sneeze. The girl takes a bite.

I finish the chicken and wash it down with beer. The beer tastes cold as it goes down, and I think that might be a line from *The Sun Also Rises.* Hemingway was always washing down his food with cold beer, and then the cold would turn warm, and he would drink another to cool down again, and he would keep drinking until a memory no longer felt like a boxer's punch to the face. All of this happened as rain fell.

There is no rain tonight. I can see a glimpse of sky, blue like jazz. My waiter approaches. I learned a couple of years ago that when an Italian waiter asks you if you want a cappuccino, he is making fun of you. Stupid Americans love cappuccino. This waiter tonight asks me if I want cappuccino. Ah, I'm on to you, signore! "No, I will have espresso," I say in Italian.

The espresso was warm. It tasted like smoke.

I pay the check and walk down the Via della Lungaretta. I see you, St. Cecilia, peeking around a corner. I run to the edge of the building, thick-walled, medieval, yellow, and decorated with flowerpots. I look right. You're not there. In the distance, I see your silhouette against a gilded mosaic wall that is hundreds of years old, but beneath the streetlamps, the image shines brightly around you (or is it you that shines brightly around everything?). I give chase, but the throat-clearing roar of a Vespa distracts me. Turning, I see an old man wearing a World War I German helmet cruising the Vespa over the cobblestones. When I look back, you're gone. In your place is a woman, a dark angel, a raven in a lace shawl. She stretches out her arms. She moves to the left, and I lose sight of her. She vanishes like a prophecy. I hear a violin, a flute, and a cello. I follow the sound, and it leads me to your church.

O, noble Cecilia, lily of heaven, patron saint of musicians, how you suffered in life. But you bring me friendship tonight. Slabs of broken marble engraved with names long gone from a world I never knew adorn an entrance to your holy home. I walk through the door and into the church. Faint music rises like incense. I look up and then to my left, and the young woman and her family from the restaurant are standing there, her shoulders now covered, showing respect for the invisible, as she arches her back, her face tan, her hair brown and gold, to stare at the ceiling of this church. A choir practices hallelujahs around an altar.

This is where heaven is.

This is life everlasting.

It's here in the way an old woman's long gray hair cascades down her back as she kneels and prays. It's here in memories late-night walks with my wife and sons on a sand-strewn boardwalk in winter. It is here among these voices tonight, penitents with heads bowed and hearts raised.

We, the fallen, get lost. Moving from thought to thought, from place to place, sometimes we stop and roll back stones only to find empty tombs. And yet, we sense something. Something. It runs through us like a swallowed needle, cutting us and creating scars. Angels and saints, sons and fathers, ghosts and mothers move through our hearts. We feel them in the muscles of our arms, the softness of our bellies, and the way a whisper enters our ears.

We believe in all that is seen and unseen. It's all the same.

St. Cecilia, I feel your presence all over. There is so much I want to tell you! I have seen life everlasting in the sound of an organ in a cathedral. I have tasted heaven in the way you look upon things. I have heard the trumpets of eternal life in my children's footfalls on creaky staircases. This is what it means. Look no further. It is here, and now, in the coldness our hands feel as they touch the marble. It is in our coughs and the pain in our feet.

Take a breath now. Hold it. Hold life everlasting in your mouth, touch it with your tongue, grind it with your teeth. Know it presses against you as you press against it.

Do you want proof of heaven? It's in the taste of salt. In an argument. In fingers that touch. In sunrises and moonsets. In the silence of a candle's flame.

I look up—a fresco of a Madonna and child. I say a prayer and turn to leave and see a mother nursing her child in a chair against a gray wall. Her skin is so white. The baby is pressed against her, its head in her hand. I smile at her, and she smiles back. Now it is here. Living paint on fresh plaster.

Outside, shadows fall on an obelisk. St. Cecilia walks with me, her spirit a hieroglyph, pointing to something I don't fully understand. This unknown something calls to me, and I want to fly. I want to grab hold of the back of an angel and soar above the drunk and lonely who walk up and down these streets tonight.

I am in love with so many tonight, with my wife and my sons back home, with the angels, who refuse to show their faces, and with you, St. Cecilia, you who are beside me one minute and running away and turning corners the next. I even love the fool talking loudly on his cell phone as a choir of human seraphim in polyester and jeans sings night prayers for all of us on the streets of this holy city.

How do we know God? Not by standing firm with puffed-out chests, not with fists, but by dissolving like sugar in coffee, salt in a pot of water, his body into hers, her body into his.

Remember, St. Cecilia says, you know an angel when its wings cast no shadow. All others are impostors.

Remember.

A bell rings, and something vibrates through me and then fades.

"Cast no shadows where you tread," St. Cecilia whispers.

"I want to go home," I say to myself.

Then like a breath in my ear, a still, small voice, not the saint's, says, "Yes, but you are home with me always."

CODA

BRUSHSTROKES

We walk unhurried
beneath the stars.
An effort to slow Time.

She is beautiful and guarded
and her laugh sparkles like glitter.
Envy the saint
who hangs 'round her neck.

Hair the color of autumn leaves.
Graceful fingers with nails like stained glass.
Cathedral eyes, and the smile of a benediction.

Side-by-side on a park bench,
their legs barely touching,
knowing the moment, sooner or later,
is going to end.

Talking to him
was like riding a bicycle over cobblestones—
What a perfect day to be someone else.

Few people
smile on the subway,
and those that do
look like lunatics.

He has the tired walk
of an old dog named Sam,
and his kid swings the bat
like a one-legged ballerina.

Standing at the gates of hell, a devil asked,
"So, what do you have to say for yourself?"
"I have a doctor's note," I replied.

The room was silent,
like a snow-covered cemetery,
or as if everyone was reading
by candlelight.

A lone country gargoyle.
Leaves in shadowed corners.
Tree branches,
bridges to nowhere.

I saw gray buildings,
soot-colored walls,
and the imagined faces of all the
people I would never meet.

A circus of memories.
Ghosts skate away.
Meet me at the Spanish City.

ABOUT THE AUTHOR

Gary Jansen is the author of several bestselling books, including the memoir *Holy Ghosts: Or, How a (Not So) Good Catholic Boy Became a Believer in Things That Go Bump in the Night*, *The 15-Minute Prayer Solution*, *Station to Station*, and the multi-award winning *MicroShifts: Transforming Your Life One Step at a Time*. His illustrated children's book, *Remember Us with Smiles*, which he co-wrote with his wife, Grace, won the 2023 Christopher Award in the Books for Young People category. His website is www.garyjansen.com.

this book is specially dedicated to

Frances Poppi
1946–2023